Sex Education or
Indoctrination?

Sex Education or Indoctrination?

How ideology has triumphed over facts

Valerie Riches

With additional research by Norman Wells

Foreword by Peter Dawson OBE

FAMILY & YOUTH CONCERN

First published as *Sex & Social Engineering* 1986
Revised and reprinted 1990
Reprinted 1994
Revised and reprinted 1999
Revised and reprinted as *Sex Education or Indoctrination?* 2004

FAMILY & YOUTH CONCERN, 2004

ISBN 0 906229 18 9

FAMILY & YOUTH CONCERN
e-mail: fyc@ukfamily.org.uk
website: www.famyouth.org.uk

Family & Youth Concern is the working title of the
Family Education Trust, a company limited by guarantee
(No 3503533) and a registered charity (No 1070500).

Printed in Great Britain by Cromwell Press, Trowbridge, Wiltshire

*If we wish to preserve the family
we must revolutionise the nation.*

G K Chesterton

Contents

About the Author

Valerie Riches is married with two children. After training as a social worker she worked with widows and their children, then with unmarried mothers. As director of Family Education Trust (Family & Youth Concern) from 1972–2000, she was a regular contributor to newspapers, magazines, radio and television programmes, speaking for parents and the family, and lectured extensively in all five continents. Having retired from the day-to-day running of the Trust, she maintains an active involvement through her role as Founder President.

About Family & Youth Concern

For the past thirty years, Family & Youth Concern (FYC) has been conducting research into the causes and consequences of family breakdown.

By means of its conferences, literature and videos, and through its media profile, FYC seeks to stimulate informed public debate on matters affecting the family. It submits evidence to parliamentary bodies, drawing on reputable research findings.

An independent research organisation, FYC does not receive government funding and is financed entirely by members' subscriptions and donations. It has no religious or political affiliations.

Foreword

Advocacy lies at the heart of all forms of sex education. There are no independents operating in the field. That is why, as Valerie Riches so rightly asserts in what follows, it is an ideological battleground.

As young people's sexuality develops and exerts an increasingly powerful influence on their behaviour, securing their commitment to a particular set of values becomes all important to those marketing newspapers and magazines; to those selling sex aids; to the music and fashion industries; to those wishing in any way to tap the enormous economic power of the teenager in the twenty-first century. Most of all, the values system that the younger generation is persuaded to adopt will have enormous political repercussions.

A fiercely determined woman once faced me across my desk as I sought to appoint a teacher to my school's human relations department. I asked her what she regarded as her aim. She said: 'I want to warn these young people against marriage'. What most worried me was her excellent record as a teacher. One would not have objected so powerfully to her being let loose on the next generation had she been hopeless in the classroom.

There are many brilliant communicators working in the field of sex education who are poisoning the minds of young people against notions of self-control and taking responsibility for the consequences of one's conduct. I once asserted on a television programme about sexual conduct that young men should not indulge in sexual activity if unready to stay and bring up any children born as a result. The studio rang with laughter at the very idea.

It is not too late to stem the tide of sexual experimentation among the young. Our society is waking up at last to the awful consequences of sex on impulse. The squadrons of pushchairs to be seen in any city centre, wheeled about by young girls depending on state benefits to survive in a cold and lonely world, testify to what the commercialisation of sex education has done.

Those who worry me most are the little boys in those pushchairs. The only model of manhood they see is their young mother's latest boyfriend, who is here today, but will very likely be gone tomorrow. What sort of men does the sex education industry think it is rearing?

The voice of Valerie Riches has warned against advocacy of 'family planning' as the panacea for society's sexual ills for many years. Hers is the voice of the prophet in the true meaning of that word. The good news is that this book, which first appeared in 1986, is now in its sixth reprinting. That reflects the deep anxiety of many people.

The key to good sex is not self-gratification and self-service but the tender loving care of one person for another. But during eight years as the leader of an Ofsted team of school inspectors, such a proposition never reached my ears. The focus of most sex education lessons had to do with what sort of contraceptives were available, and how to obtain a sufficient supply for one's teenage needs. The glorious future promise of the morning-after pill being made available from the school nurse was frequently offered.

The great boxer and defender of human rights we know as Mohammed Ali once said, when questioned about his beliefs: 'I don't always know what I'm talking about, but I know I'm right.' You don't have to be any kind of expert in the field of human sexuality to know what is right, so let's not be dazzled by the verbal dexterity of those attempting to market what they call sexual freedom, but which is in fact freedom for themselves to manipulate the minds of the young.

The relationship between the sexes is the most powerful force in all creation. It holds within its compass the very continuation of society. It is not to be reduced to mechanisms that promote enjoyment without responsibility. That is the essence of Valerie Riches' message. We ignore it at our peril.

Peter Dawson, OBE

Executive Summary

- During the late 1960s and early 1970s, a network of government-funded pressure groups began to pursue a broad agenda covering eugenics, population control, sexual and family law reform, sex and health education, and children's rights. The thrust of their campaign was the separation of sexual activity from childbearing and from marriage. The launch of the contraceptive pill in 1961 facilitated the former. The latter required a major change in social norms.

- Sex education in schools has become an ideological battlefield on which war is waged for the hearts and minds of children. The parental right to withdraw children from sex education has been strongly opposed by government-funded groups. Attempts to limit the antinomian activities of such groups by parliament have failed, because terms such as 'moral considerations' and 'family life' have been interpreted so broadly as to rob them of any meaning.

- The most insidious 'reform' has been the elimination of parents from decisions that vitally affect their children's lives. The first and most important of the policy changes in this respect was the provision of contraceptives to underage children without the knowledge or consent of their parents.

- Parents have struggled to regain responsibility for their children's welfare via the courts and parliament. The deliberately wide interpretation by teen-sex lobbyists of both court rulings and legislation has rendered most of these attempts ineffective. The 'medicalisation' of the response by schools to teenage sexuality has succeeded in reducing the small amount of control which parents might have been able to exercise.

- The Teenage Pregnancy Unit was set up by the government to reduce the UK's teenage pregnancy rate – the highest in Western Europe. Its policy is based on strategies which have been shown to be ineffective, in particular widening access to contraception for young teens and giving them more explicit sex education. The official response to what is widely acknowledged as a crisis in the sexual health of young people remains the promotion of the condom, in spite of the fact that it gives only limited protection against some sexually transmitted infections, particularly for girls.

- The obvious alternative of encouraging abstinence in teenagers has been greeted with hostility in both official and semi-official circles.

- The hostility to abstinence education and the support for failed policies can only be understood in terms of the ideology embraced by those who wish to change social structures and replace parental influence by the authority of the state. As Helen Brook so succinctly put it:

  'It is now the privilege of the Parental State to take major decisions – objective, unemotional, the State weighs up what is best for the child.' [1]

---

[1] Letter to the Editor, *The Times*, 16 February 1980, also see p.31.

Introduction

It is now, unfortunately, only too well known that Britain has the highest teenage pregnancy rate in Western Europe. Official concern about this reached such levels towards the end of the 1990s that the Prime Minister set up a Teenage Pregnancy Unit (TPU) charged with the mission of halving the under-18 conception rate by 2010.

This was an aim behind which the Prime Minister could reasonably expect the nation to unite. We may have different views about sex outside of marriage, cohabitation, divorce and other issues affecting the family, but no reasonable person of any political persuasion thinks that it is a good idea for teenage girls, who in some cases are scarcely more than children themselves, to be bringing babies into the world. The evidence of the disadvantages suffered by both mothers and babies in such circumstances is overwhelming. We all want to prevent these unfortunate situations from occurring.

Alas, those of us who believed the rhetoric about bold and radical new approaches to the subject were dismayed when we saw what the TPU was actually proposing. It amounted to more sex education at younger ages, and more provision of contraception to teenagers, including underage teens, without their parents' knowledge or consent.

Far from being bold or radical, these are the policy responses which have been in place for the last thirty years, with a conspicuous lack of success. Given that the current buzzword is 'evidence-based' – as in evidence-based policies – it is difficult to understand why policies which have never been shown to be effective, and which may even be counter-productive, should be endlessly recycled, whichever party is in government.

This is an area in which the ideology trumps the research every time. You only have to listen to the way in which the issue is debated – or more strikingly, to the way in which the chief public proponents of the policy have refused to debate their stance at all – to know that this is not an area in which serious research is ever going to be heeded. People have their own convictions, and are going to hold onto them, no matter what.

I have written elsewhere about the effects of the policy of providing contraception to young girls behind their parents' backs.[2] In this pamphlet I want to look at the issue of sex education, that form of instruction on which officials pin such high hopes, in spite of the fact that there is no serious research, from anywhere in the world, to indicate that the sort of early, permissive sex education they advocate could ever reduce conception rates. But it has never really been about education. Sex education bears the same relation to education as voodoo bears to medicine, or astrology to astronomy. It rests on faith, not facts.

My interest in the subject of school sex education arose from my own family's experience, when one of our children, aged fourteen, came home from school one day overwhelmed by the content of a sex education lesson which had been given by the biology teacher, fresh from a training course run by the Family Planning Association. The full range of contraceptives had been demonstrated to the students with the message that party-going inevitably led to sexual intercourse, and that a means of birth control was therefore a prerequisite. If, however, a pregnancy resulted, an abortion could always be arranged.

My husband and I regarded this message not only as an attack on our parental beliefs and responsibilities but as a blatant encouragement to promiscuity. Yet our complaint to the school was summarily dismissed as if our views were of no

---

[2] Valerie Riches, *Who Cares for Children? The implications of providing birth control for under-sixteens*, Family & Youth Concern, 1989.

consequence. Thus it was that we began to ask questions. Why the contempt for parents' opinions and mores? Why, despite all the sex education and free availability of contraceptives, were unwanted pregnancies, abortions and sexually transmitted infections rising? Why was sex education, unlike other subjects in the school curriculum, introduced without the provision of an impartial academic body to assess and evaluate the success or failure of the methodology applied? How had it all come about?

The more we investigated, the more we were astonished by what we unearthed and the extent to which we had ourselves been influenced by the prevailing liberal assumptions. It was therefore as a concerned parent and social worker that in 1970 I became involved with a new venture which was to become known as Family & Youth Concern (FYC).[3] This was established by doctors, teachers and social workers who saw the need to analyse the social influences which were giving rise to family breakdown and the emotional and physical manifestations caused by the ravages of permissive lifestyles.

FYC has no political or religious affiliations. It supports responsible family planning in its proper context for the spacing and timing of children in marriage, as a personal decision for couples to make in accordance with their cultural and religious beliefs. It also believes that parents, or known and respected figures, are the appropriate people to impart information and values to children about their developing sexuality. When sex education is given in schools, we urge that it should be dealt with sensitively by people of integrity, with the full co-operation of parents and with the aim of preparing young people for their future roles in marriage and parenthood. We consider it essential that children should be protected from exposure to types of sex instruction which are amoral in content, and which erode known

---

[3] Family & Youth Concern is the working title of the Family Education Trust, a registered charity and independent think-tank which publishes research into the causes and effects of family breakdown.

3

and tried human values that have evolved over thousands of years as safeguards of the social order.

It must be recognised that not all those people associated with the organisations mentioned in the following pages have sinister intentions. There are doubtless many who are motivated by idealism, unaware that they are actually supporting a destructive agenda laid down by a relatively small number of radical men and women, whose driving force is a mixture of new-found ideology, power and economics.

This publication reveals some of the forces involved in a concerted attempt to alter the future destiny of the family through the sex education of children in schools. It began as a paper written for a lecture tour of New Zealand in 1982, explaining the research I had carried out into the origins and development of school-based sex education. This was published in booklet form in 1986, and the need for the information it contained quickly became apparent as requests to speak on the subject came from all five continents. Tens of thousands of copies have been printed in a dozen different languages and it has been necessary to bring the publication up to date from time to time. I am greatly indebted to Norman Wells for the immense amount of detailed work he has carried out in bringing together the latest research and political policies for inclusion in this new edition, and to Robert Whelan for his editorial assistance.

I trust that it will alert parents, policy makers and governments, and help them to recognise that the assault on the family is not simply a national phenomenon, but an issue now facing countries around the world. It is to be hoped that when the nature, size and urgency of the problem is fully understood, then the energy will be found to discover solutions.

Valerie Riches
January 2004

Chapter 1

The network

In the late 1960s and early 1970s, there were numerous intensive political campaigns emanating from a nexus of organisations in the field of birth control (i.e. contraception, sterilisation and abortion). From an analysis of their annual reports it became apparent that a comparatively small number of people was involved to a surprising degree in an array of pressure groups. This network was not only linked by personnel, but by funds, ideology and sometimes shared addresses. It was also backed by vested interests and supported with grants from various government departments. At the heart of the network was the Family Planning Association (FPA) with its own collection of offshoots. It was a power structure with enormous influence.

Further investigation revealed that the network had a wider agenda, covering eugenics, population control, sexual and family law reforms, sex and health education, and children's rights. Its tentacles reached out to publishing houses, medical, educational and research establishments, women's organisations and marriage guidance services. It appeared to have great influence over the media and over permanent officials in relevant government departments, out of all proportion to the numbers involved, with international implications which were not immediately appreciated.

During the early 1970s, a booklet was published with the intriguing title *The Men Behind Hitler: A German Warning to the World.*[4] Its thesis was that the eugenics movement, which had gained popularity early in the twentieth century, had gone underground following the holocaust in Nazi Germany, but was

---

[4] Bernard Schreiber, *The Men Behind Hitler*, La Haye, Mureaux, France.

5

still active and functioning through organisations promoting abortion, euthanasia, sterilisation and mental health. The author urged readers to look at their home countries and neighbouring countries, for they would surely find that members and committees of these organisations would cross-check to a remarkable extent.

Other books and papers from independent sources later confirmed that this was the case. From Africa came *All Kinds of Family Planning*;[5] from Colombia, *The Structure of Genocide*;[6] and from France, *Un Complot Contre La Vie*.[7] The latter, a carefully documented book, discussed the geopolitics of abortion and population control as a means of exerting worldwide power by a handful of the 'richest of the rich' who felt threatened by the rising power of the poor nations due to their sheer numbers and slow but steady economic progress.

A remarkable book was also published in America which documented the activities of the Sex Information and Education Council of the United States (SIECUS). It was entitled *The SIECUS Circle: A Humanist Revolution*.[8] SIECUS was set up in 1964 and lost no time in engaging in a programme of social engineering by means of sex education in schools. Its first executive director was Mary Calderone, who was also closely linked to Planned Parenthood, the American equivalent of the British FPA. According to *The SIECUS Circle*, Calderone supported sentiments and theories put forward by Rudolph Dreikus, a humanist, such as:

---

[5] Michael Golden, *All Kinds of Family Planning*, African Universities Press, 1981.

[6] Varlos Utirsi Otalora and Marfa Cristina de Corsi, *The Structure of Genocide*, Bogota, Columbia, 1981.

[7] Emerentienne de Lagrange, Marguerita-Marie de Lagrange and René Bel, *Un Complot contre la Vie*, Société de Production Litteraire, 1979.

[8] Claire Chambers, *The SIECUS Circle, A Humanist Revolution*, Western Islands, 1977.

- merging or reversing the sexes or sex roles;
- liberating children from their families;
- abolishing the family as we know it.[9]

Even though the authors of these books had begun their investigations from different angles, their shared conclusion was that there is a carefully planned international attack upon the nature of the family and the value of human life, with roots going back almost two hundred years.

The Fear of People

The population control movement had its origins in the *Essay on the Principle of Population*, written by the Rev. Thomas Malthus in 1798, in which he argued that the population would always increase at a faster rate than the food supply, and that the result would be an increase in poverty, misery and vice. The only solution he was able to propose was sexual abstinence for the poor.[10]

Charles Darwin came across Malthus' essay when he was writing *The Origin of the Species* and began to extend the scope of his work from the animal kingdom to include mankind. He believed that civilised societies weakened themselves by misplaced compassion:

> With savages, the weak in mind or body are soon eliminated . . . We civilised men, on the other hand . . . build asylums for the imbecile, the maimed and the sick; we institute poor laws; and our medical men exert their utmost skill to save the life of everyone to the last moment . . . Thus the weak members of civilised societies propagate their kind. No one who has ever

---

[9] *Ibid* p.14.

[10] Thomas R Malthus, *An essay on the principle of population*, London, 1798.

attended to the breeding of domestic animals will doubt that this must be highly injurious to the race of man.[11]

Darwin's cousin, Frances Galton, was a psychologist who enthusiastically embraced Darwin's ideas and used them to formulate the 'science' of eugenics. This is the belief that certain people are of a superior strain, and that the race can be improved by breeding selectively from them.

The question which immediately occupied the eugenicists was, how do you stop those of inferior strains from breeding and damaging the racial stock? This marked the beginning of the birth control movement.

The two most influential campaigners for birth control, Marie Stopes in England and Margaret Sanger in America, were both racists and eugenicists whose primary interest in birth control lay not in assisting women to space their children, but in the prevention of births to groups in society considered by them to be undesirable. Marie Stopes wrote:

> Society allows the diseased, the racially negligent, the thriftless, the careless, the feeble minded, the very lowest and worst members of the community to produce innumerable tens of thousands of stunted, warped, inferior infants . . . a large proportion of these are doomed from their very physical inheritance to be at best but partly self-supporting, and thus to drain the resources of those classes above them who have a sense of responsibility. The better classes, freed from the cost of institutions, hospitals, prisons and so on, principally filled by the inferior racial stock, would be able to afford to enlarge their own families.

As an answer to this problem she advocated:

---

[11] Charles Darwin, *The Descent of Man*, London, 1871.

The sterilisation of those totally unfit for parenthood to be made an immediate possibility, indeed made compulsory.[12]

Margaret Sanger, the founder of Planned Parenthood Federation of America, coined the slogan 'Birth Control, to create a race of thoroughbreds'.[13] Sharing Stopes' concern about the breeding habits of those she deemed 'least fit to carry on the race', she drew up a 'Plan for Peace', which included the following recommendations:

- to apply a stern and rigid policy of sterilisation and segregation to that grade of population whose progeny is already tainted, or whose inheritance is such that objectionable traits may be transmitted to offspring.

- to apportion farmlands and homesteads for these segregated persons where they would be taught to work under competent instructors for the period of their entire lives.[14]

Neither Stopes nor Sanger had much chance of achieving their mass sterilisation programmes in the free societies in which they lived, and both detested democracy as a result. However the rise to power of the Nazi party in 1933, with its emphasis on racial purity, finally gave the eugenicists the chance to put their theories into practice.

The Nazi programme to breed a master race moved swiftly from mass sterilisation programmes, through euthanasia of the physically and mentally handicapped, to the concentration camps in which over six million men, women and children regarded as genetically inferior were sent to the gas chambers.

After the war, when the truth about these programmes emerged, the eugenics movement had to go underground, and

---

[12] Marie Stopes, *Radiant Motherhood*, London, 1920.

[13] Margaret Sanger, *Birth Control Review*, December 1921.

[14] Margaret Sanger, *Birth Control Review*, April 1932.

the term 'birth control', which had strong Nazi connotations, was dropped in favour of 'family planning'. Eugenicists and birth controllers had to find a new justification for their activities. The novel idea that the world was overpopulated gave them their justification. The population control movement was born.

A Blueprint for the Sexual Revolution

For nearly two thousand years in the Western world there had been a basic commitment to the ideal, if not always the practice, of associating sex with love and faithfulness in the context of monogamous marriage. However, towards the middle of the twentieth century great changes took place, quite different in nature from previous periods of permissive sexual behaviour. Among the most obvious contributing factors to this change were the Kinsey Reports published in 1948 and 1953, financed by the Rockefeller Foundation.[15]

Alfred C. Kinsey, a biologist, applied to over 12,000 humans the techniques he had used in studying gall wasps. From the data he collected, he proved to his satisfaction that there was no such thing as 'normality' or 'abnormality' in sexual behaviour; no 'rights and wrongs'. The validity of Kinsey's sampling techniques was challenged as soon as the first volume of the report appeared. The respondents were not a random sample of the population, but volunteers. It was only too evident that the results depended absolutely on the type of person who volunteered.

In spite of the inadequacies of the methods employed by Kinsey, the claims made in his reports quickly came to be treated as fact and were used by the media, 'sexual minorities' and groups with vested interests as an excuse for sexual

---

[15] A. C. Kinsey, *Sexual Behaviour in the Human Male*, Saunders, Pa., 1948; *Sexual Behaviour in the Human Female*, Saunders, Pa., 1953.

freedom. Sex became a commodity to be exploited, and love a subject to be avoided. The flaws in Kinsey's method have since been exposed: around one quarter of the male sample had comprised prisoners, including several hundred male prostitutes, and children as young as two months had been sexually stimulated to show that sexual activity could be enjoyed from infancy. Data collected from criminal sources was thus presented as serious scientific research.[16] Nevertheless, it is impossible to underestimate the far-reaching influence these oft-quoted reports have had on sexual attitudes, sexual behaviour and sex education policies. The Kinsey reports provided the blueprint for the sex education missionaries - and the long-term effects on Western societies are obvious.

The Ideology of Chisholm

There is no better example of the ideology lying behind the pressures for sex education than that contained in *Can People Learn to Learn?* by Dr Brock Chisholm. A humanist, he served as first director of the World Health Organisation and subsequently president of the World Federation for Mental Health.[17]

Chisholm was wedded to the idea of world government, and believed that those who opposed him were neurotic, selfish or mentally ill. He was persuaded that the most persistent barrier to developing a civilised way of life in the world was the concept of 'right and wrong', a concept which he thought should be eradicated. Codes of belief, fixed rules or dogmatism, were anathema to him. Children had to be freed from national, religious and other cultural 'prejudices' forced upon them by parents and religious authorities. He saw parents as dictators and suppressors of the child's better nature, and believed that sex

---

[16] Judith A Reisman and E W Eichel, *Kinsey, Sex and Fraud, The Indoctrination of a People*, edited by John H Court and J Gordon Muir, Huntingdon House, 1990.

[17] Brock Chisholm, *Can People Learn to Learn?* Geo. Allen and Unwin, 1958.

11

education should be introduced from the age of nine, eliminating 'the ways of elders' – by force if necessary.[18] Chisholm's ideology is deeply embedded in the thinking of the sex education lobby and is reflected in many radical sex education publications and materials.

---

[18] Brock Chisholm, 'The Psychiatry of Enduring Peace and Social Progress', *Psychiatry*, Vol 9, 1946.

Chapter 2

The International
Planned Parenthood Federation

In 1952 Margaret Sanger founded the International Planned
Parenthood Federation (IPPF), a body dedicated to the
advancement and acceptance of family planning throughout the
world, with its headquarters in London. The eight founding
member associations included the British Family Planning
Association and the Planned Parenthood Federation of America.
The same year saw the foundation of the Population Council in
New York, with the aim of providing solid scientific evidence to
guide governments and individuals in addressing population
questions and 'to improve the quality of people's lives, to help
make it possible for individuals everywhere to develop their full
potential'.[19] The Council's founder, John D. Rockefeller III, was
instrumental in persuading the United Nations to commit itself
to population control.

Population Control via Sex Education
Both the Population Council and the IPPF were and are
extremely active in devising and implementing a massive
campaign for the acceptance of contraceptive technology.

The contraceptive pill was Margaret Sanger's brainchild.
She established the Margaret Sanger Bureau which financed its
development. It was the introduction of the pill in 1960 which
put contraception on the map universally. Women were assured
that now at last they had the freedom to control their fertility;

---

[19] http://www.popcouncil.org/pc50/Panels/Historytext.html

sexual intercourse could be separated completely from reproduction. They were told it was 'safe' and 100% reliable.

It is not difficult to estimate the profits the pill represents for the pharmaceutical industry. Nor is it difficult to imagine how important the advent of the pill was to the sexual revolutionaries and the sex educators and their plans for a brave new world.

However, after a time of trial and reflection, it became known – though not necessarily to the consumer – that the new wonder drug was not so safe or reliable, but involved considerable health risks. But those who dared to publicise the problems associated with the pill or its potential hazards when prescribed for adolescent girls were immediately branded as liars, scaremongers or in league with the Pope.

There is also a worldwide campaign to promote abortion and 'temporary' or permanent sterilisation, following the 'failure' of the Third World to use contraception effectively. The campaign for population control entails a great deal else, as we shall see. The fact is that IPPF currently links national family planning associations in over 180 countries worldwide with interests that go far beyond the provision of family planning services to the underdeveloped countries.

In 1976, IPPF set out its *Strategy of Legal Reform – and How FPAs are Interpreting It.*[20] It was clear from this that IPPF requires national family planning associations to find sources of law and arguments upon which to base reforms – reforms not confined to family planning services. Under the general heading of 'the status of women' the reforms envisaged include women's rights to abortion, a lower age of consent for birth control services 'to meet the needs of young people' and, of course, compulsory sex education.

---

[20] *Strategy for Legal Reform and How FPAs are interpreting it,* IPPF News, July/August 1976.

14

Eight years later, in its report, *The Human Right to Family Planning,* IPPF went even further when it asserted that:

> Family Planning Associations and other non-governmental organisations should not use the absence of law or the existence of an unfavourable law as an excuse for inaction; actions outside the law, and *even in violation of it,* is part of the process of stimulating change.[21] (emphasis added)

To achieve its aims IPPF also encourages the formation of a climate of public opinion in which governments can be persuaded to accept responsibility for birth control services. And, as governments respond by funding programmes, IPPF affiliates provide a nucleus of staff around which the birth control services can be built. These staff train personnel (including government staff), and in this way IPPF's activities are integrated with government programmes and maximum control is assured.[22] This explains why in Britain we meet evasion and prevarication when we approach government officials about the activities of IPPF and the FPA.

IPPF's publications frequently emphasise the need to reach out to young people and implement approaches to population awareness, family life and sex education.[23] The books and sex education aids recommended for the young by IPPF, however, have little to do with family life. Chisholm's ideology is more apparent: no 'rights and wrongs', no barriers to sexual activity other than the insistence on contraceptive usage. Paradoxically, this is an approach to sex which encourages in the young the very activity which one might imagine such education should

---

[21] *The Human Right to Family Planning,* IPPF, 1984 (cf. also *The Voluntary Sector in Population and Development,* IPPF, 1979).

[22] *Her Future in the Balance* (pamphlet), IPPF, 1971.

[23] *Selected Resource Materials: Approaches to Population Awareness, Family Life and Sex Education for Young People,* IPPF, March 1978.

15

discourage as inimical to population control, *viz.* increased sexual activity.

The population control movement now admits that the main influence on couples' attitudes to fertility is not the availability of contraception or abortion, but the culture in which they live. Since most cultures are centred on the family, if family size in developing countries is to be brought closer to the very small and even childless families which are common in Western and developed countries, people in those countries must be made to conform to the assumptions and values of modern Western consumer societies. Amongst the key assumptions are: that sex and marriage, and sex and childbearing, do not need to go together; that cohabitation is a viable, even desirable alternative to marriage; and that children have a right to their own sex lives without interference from their parents.

When such attitudes are adopted, birth rates fall. Hence the attack on the family which always forms part of sex education programmes instigated or influenced by the population control movement. To understand more fully the implications of the type of sex education that the population controllers promote, the chart on pages 18–19 is enlightening. It was originally sent by Frederick S. Jaffé, Vice President of Planned Parenthood/World Population, to Bernard Berelson, former president of the Population Council. Berelson obviously took these proposals seriously for he included many of them, and even more radical ones, in a chilling speech entitled 'Beyond Family Planning', delivered at the Population Conference in Dacca in 1969.[24] Among his ideas some familiar themes occurred: the inclusion of population materials in primary and secondary schools; direct manipulation of family structure; the promotion of two types of marriage, one childless and readily

---

[24] Bernard Berelson, *Beyond Family Planning*, Population Control Conference Paper, Dacca, 1969.

dissolved, the other licensed for children and designed to be stable.

A number of the proposals set out by Jaffé and Berelson have already been implemented in Britain, sometimes through the back door:

- Compulsory sex education in secondary schools
- Sex education which tends to emphasise that homosexual activity is normal and natural.
- Payments to doctors to provide contraception, abortion and sterilisation services.
- The 1967 Abortion Act which allows *de facto* abortion on demand as a woman's right, without the consent of the husband or partner.
- A free contraceptive service for all, irrespective of marital status, and regardless of age.
- The right of underage children to contraception and abortion without parental consent.
- A series of divorce law reforms culminating in no-fault divorce.
- The definition of the moment when human life commences has been changed from fertilisation to implantation, thus permitting the ready availability of post-coital 'contraception'.

There is relentless propaganda through the media to encourage women to work outside the home, to postpone or avoid marriage, and to regard the ideal family as two children (or less) on the grounds that children are costly and inhibiting.

Campaign Techniques

The campaign techniques which have been employed to bring about these reforms have been methodical and effective. They are recognisable in other countries where similar campaigns

Examples of proposed measures to reduce

Universal impact

Social Constraints

Restructure family:

a) Postpone or avoid
   marriage
b) Alter image of
   ideal family

Compulsory education
of children

Percentage increased
homosexuality

Educate for family limitation

Healthy control agents
in water supply

Encourage women to work

Selective impact depending on socio-economic status

Economic Deterrents / Incentives

Modify tax policies

a) Substantial marriage tax
b) Child tax
c) Tax married more than single
d) Remove parents' tax exemption
e) Additional taxes on parents with
   more than one or two children at
   school

Reduce / eliminate paid
maternity leave or benefits

Reduce / eliminate children's
or family allowances

Bonuses for delayed marriages and
greater child spacing

Pensions for women of 45
with less than N children

Eliminate welfare payments after
first two children

Chronic depression

Require women to work and
provide few childcare facilities

U.S. fertility by universality or selectivity of impact

Limit / eliminate public financed medical care, scholarships, housing, loans and subsidies to families with more than N children

Social Controls

Compulsory abortion of out-of-wedlock pregnancies

Compulsory sterilization of all who have two children except for a few who would be allowed three

Confine childbearing to only a limited number of adults

Stock certificate-type permits for children

Housing Policies

a) Discouragement of private home ownership

b) Stop awarding public housing based on family size

Measures predicated on existing motivation to prevent unwanted pregnancy

Payments to encourage sterilization

Payments to encourage contraception

Payments to encourage abortion

Abortion and sterilization on demand

Allow certain contraceptives to be distributed non-medically

Improve contraceptive technology

Make contraception truly available and accessible to all

Improve maternal healthcare, with family planning as a core element

---

The author of this chart was Frederick Jaffé,
Vice President of Planned Parenthood /World Population
Source: *Activities Relevant to the Study of Population Policy for the U.S.*
Memorandum from Frederick S Jaffé to Bernard Berelson, 11 March 1969

have taken place. Having developed legal arguments, however specious, upon which to base the reforms, IPPF affiliates set up groups with appealing titles to put pressure on their parliaments.

'Hard cases' are often used to soften up public opinion. For example, 'Fourteen-year-old girl dies after giving birth in churchyard' is ideal headline material to sensationalise the cause. Slogans are used widely, like 'every child a wanted child', 'safe sex for teenagers', 'meeting the needs of young people' and 'the right to confidentiality', to suggest that if underage girls were given FPA-type sex education, with free access to contraceptives without fear of their parents knowing, they would not end up pregnant. Following such spurious propaganda we are then confronted with proposals, articles, research and studies to reinforce the arguments, none of which bears too much scrutiny for scientific validity.

With monotonous regularity, a range of women's magazines joins in the campaign with surveys which are presented to the public as scientific fact. However, the participants are volunteer readers of the magazines, not a representative sample of the population.

There is publicity value in inflated statistics too. As Dr Malcolm Potts, the international spokesman on population control, has said: 'Those who want the [abortion] law to be liberalised will claim that hundreds or thousands of women die unnecessarily each year, when the actual number is far lower'.[25]

Two examples will suffice: in France, figures were circulated to reinforce the campaign for a liberalised abortion law. It was said that 1.5 million or even 2.5 million clandestine abortions took place annually. The official French statistical organisation INED, however, prudently challenged these figures, and estimated in a report that the number of illegally induced abortions was 250,000. But even this figure included

---

[25] Malcolm Potts, *Abortion*, Cambridge University Press, 1977

20

all deaths from obstetric origins for one year (1963), as if all such deaths were due to abortion. In another section of the French report, the researchers erroneously added into the equation figures from a column of *male* deaths instead of *female* deaths from 'indeterminate or unknown causes' between the ages of 15-49, and assumed them to be caused by abortion. This had the effect of doubling the number of illegal abortions recorded. So it appears that in France, men not only could become pregnant, they could also die from abortions![26]

In Portugal, the figure of 2,000 deaths from illegal abortions each year was publicised. In fact the UN Demographic Year Book for 1975 gave the figure of only 2099 female deaths from *all causes* in the main childbearing years.

IPPF Youth Manifesto

During 1998, the Youth Committee of IPPF developed a manifesto to meet 'the sexual and reproductive health needs of young people' at the dawn of the new millennium, and to promote 'the partnership of young people and adults to ensure that young people can make informed choices and enjoy their sexuality'. Entitled *ippf/youth*, the core values of the manifesto include 'freedom of sexual expression', 'free[dom] from judgement', 'confidentiality', 'respect for diversity', 'sexual enjoyment', and access to contraceptive services for all young people'.[27]

The document calls for the promotion of 'sexual pleasure as a valid sexual and reproductive health need for all young people including those living with HIV/AIDS, and young people with disabilities'. It also insists that 'laws that allow young people to act freely in the way they choose to live their lives' will be required in order to meet the goal of giving young people

---

[26] Emerenienne de Lagrange *et al*, *op. cit.*

[27] http://www.ippf.org/resource/youth/report98/manifesto.htm

'pleasure and confidence in relationships and all aspects of sexuality'.

The manifesto was presented to the IPPF Youth Parliament meeting in Prague in November 1998 and financially supported by IPPF and the United Nations Population Fund. Having been endorsed by the Parliament, consisting of 43 young people from 38 countries, the manifesto was referred to IPPF's Central Council, which passed resolutions committing both ideological and practical support. The printed document states that IPPF's member family planning associations are working hard to ensure that the vision of the manifesto becomes a reality throughout the world.

There is no reference anywhere in the manifesto to parental responsibilities, child protection issues, nor even the age at which young people are held to acquire their 'sexual rights'. 'Non-judgementalism' apparently has no limits as far as the manifesto is concerned. It extends to all regardless of marital status, sexual lifestyle and even age, given that the IPPF includes under the designation 'young people' everyone between the ages of 10 and 24, according to the accepted usage of the World Health Organisation.

The kind of sexual and reproductive health education programmes envisaged are to be complemented by 'youth centres and youth clinics providing a complete range of sexual and reproductive health services including contraceptive provision for all young people'.

In an 'urgent alert on children's rights' issued in advance of the World Summit for Children which had been scheduled for September 2001, the IPPF's European Network called on its affiliates to campaign for a strong statement in the outcome document 'to guarantee full access of adolescents to sexual and reproductive health information, education and services'. Concern was expressed that 'right-wing' organisations were promoting the family based on marriage as the ideal 'despite the fact...that many families are neither safe, particularly for young girls, nor models of gender equality'. The document proceeded to argue that children's rights must take precedence over parental authority and that education in sexual abstinence should be resisted:

> Right-wing governments and groups are also attempting to insert language in the outcome document that would strengthen parental authority and control to the detriment of established children's rights. For instance, they are calling for language to be included to the effect that HIV/AIDS counselling for children and adolescents would only be available with the 'knowledge of parents', and generally oppose providing information, education and services to adolescents with respect to their sexual and reproductive health and rights, without parental consent. Clearly, the adoption of such language must be fought against as it could result in significant damage to young people's access to reproductive health services.
>
> Of great concern is the fact that right-wing organisations are aggressively promoting the idea that 'instead of teaching children how to protect themselves from HIV/AIDS, we should teach them the culture of chastity and self-control'.[28]

No country which believes in democracy should ignore the power and influence of IPPF working through its national family planning associations to instigate policies and laws which are damaging to parental authority and the structure of the family, and indeed to the health and welfare of young people.

---

[28] Karin Helsacke, 'Urgent Alert on Children's Rights', IPPF European Network, undated.

23

Chapter 3

The FPA and sex education in schools

In 1921 Dr Marie Stopes founded a birth control clinic in London from which evolved the National Birth Control Council. In 1939 the Council changed its name to the Family Planning Association and became a veritable pillar of respectability in British society. However, profound changes were to take place.

In 1976, after the FPA had relinquished most of its clinics to area health authorities, it concentrated its efforts on population control, sex education and providing information for the government on birth control services. Among its targets for the future were the provision of 'suitable programmes for sex education in schools throughout the UK' and 'a volunteer youth movement throughout Britain which is able to put young people in touch with sound advice on sexual problems'.[29]

The FPA's sex education activities are intrinsic to the central theme outlined earlier: a perfect example of Chisholmism. They sow confusion in the child's mind about the validity of the concept of right and wrong and present only one moral absolute: the use of contraceptives 'every time you have sex'. Lying darkly beneath the persuasive contraceptive propaganda fed to children is a sinister attitude towards birth. The misery of the unwanted child is stressed. For example, a leaflet issued by Population Concern, an offshoot of the FPA, carried the caption: 'There's one born every quarter of a second'. The association of the birth of a baby with the expression about a fool being born every minute is unmistakable.

---

[29] Family Planning Association Annual Report 1977/8.

Far-reaching Influence

The power of the FPA to influence thinking, teaching and policy-making at every level of British society is far-reaching. It is achieved directly through representation in political circles on committees of national organisations, and indirectly through the media, over which the FPA has considerable influence. The FPA also has its own offshoots through which its strategy for reforms can be achieved:

- The Brook Advisory Centre was set up in 1964 to provide contraceptives and, subsequently, to arrange abortions for the young. Its manifesto, *Safe Sex for Teenagers*, made clear its policy on providing contraception; that 'the customer is always right' and that it never reported men who broke the law by having intercourse with underage girls.[30]

- Population Concern was set up in 1962 as a joint project of the Family Planning Association and the Simon Population Trust. Originally known as the Family Planning International Campaign and later renamed Countdown, it served as a fund-raising body to channel funds to IPPF and the FPA to promote their sex education activities.[31] In 1991 it received independent charitable status and is now known as Interact Worldwide.[32]

- Family Planning Sales Ltd (FP Sales) was set up in 1972 to distribute contraceptives and other family planning materials to GPs and family planning clinics throughout the UK and to provide a contraceptive mail order service. Until March 2002, when it was purchased by Williams Medical Supplies, it was

---

[30] *Safe Sex For Teenagers*, Brook Advisory Centres, London, 1978.

[31] *http://library.wellcome.ac.uk/collections/am_sub_socm2r.shtml*

[32] *http://www.populationconcern.org.uk/*

wholly owned by the FPA, and the 2003 FP Sales contraceptive catalogue still advises customers that 'every order placed with FP Sales Ltd financially benefits FPA'. The company accounts for 2002 record that £374,537 was due to be paid to the Family Planning Association.

With the assistance of public funding, the FPA also provides courses for the training of teachers, youth leaders, social workers, doctors and others. In 1974, the Association issued a statement on sex education which said that one of the FPA's goals was to create a society in which 'archaic sex laws and irrational fears of sex and sex exploitation are non-existent'.[33]

Throughout the 1970s, the FPA enthusiastically supported every radical book that came on to the market, including *The Little Red School Book*, later judged obscene by the courts. Another book, *Sex Education, the Erroneous Zone*, published by the National Secular Society, was promoted by the FPA. This advised that economic freedom would give girls the ability to choose as many lovers as they wished, of either sex. It also suggested oral and anal intercourse as methods of contraception, a suggestion which occurs more and more often in sex education publications for the young.

The FPA was also involved in 1978 with the promotion of *Make It Happy*, by the secretary of the Sexual Law Reform Society, Jane Cousins. This book seeks to undermine laws and social constraints which regulate sexual behaviour in any civilised society. Oral and anal intercourse, group sex, communal masturbation, incest between brothers and sisters, and sexual contact with animals short of actual coupling are put forward, with the suggestion that those who oppose such activities are old-fashioned and killjoys.[34]

---

[33] *Sex Education, An FPA Statement*, August, 1974

[34] Jane Cousins, *Make It Happy*, Virago, 1978.

Taught Not Caught: Strategies for Sex Education was originally produced by an Australian feminist collective. The British edition was recommended by the Family Planning Association, and co-authored by a member of the FPA's Education Unit. One section for teachers is entitled *What is appropriate behaviour?* The aim is 'to increase tolerance towards a range of expressions of sexuality'. Sixteen-year-olds are asked to discuss the following situations:

- Parents are in bed together having sexual intercourse when their three-year-old enters the room. They include the child in their embrace.

- A mother is changing her baby son's nappy. He shows by giggling that he enjoys having his penis touched. She continues to touch him all over, including the penis.

- A boy sits on his grandfather's knee. Grandfather strokes his hair.

Taught Not Caught was published at a time of great public concern over the rising incidence of reported cases of the sexual abuse of children. The attitudes it encourages would do nothing to mitigate this problem.[35]

Sex Education Material

Much of the sex education material currently available to young people describes sexual intercourse in terms of 'boy' and 'girl' activity, rather than 'husband' and 'wife'. It is difficult to find any mention of marriage as a positive relationship to aim for. Facts about the medically established link between early sexual intercourse or sex with multiple partners and cancer of the cervix are glossed over, as are the side effects of the pill and of abortion. While rising rates of sexually transmitted infections (STIs) among young people have become a matter of serious

---

[35] The Clarity Collective, *Taught Not Caught*, Learning Development Aids, 1985

27

public health concern, the emphasis has been on early treatment and risk reduction through condom usage rather than on eliminating risk altogether. The impression is given that sexual intercourse unavoidably carries with it the risk of contracting an STI, but that early medical intervention will generally be able to resolve the problem.

For example, an FPA 'beginner's guide to sexually transmitted infections' assures young people that STIs do not discriminate and that everyone who has sex is at risk:

> You don't need to have a lot of sexual partners to get a sexually transmitted infection (STI). Anybody who has sex – male, female, straight, gay, lesbian – can get one... Most STIs can be cured if found early enough.[36]

Nowhere is there any mention that sexual intercourse within the context of a faithful, monogamous, lifelong heterosexual relation-ship carries no risk of contracting an STI. The avoidance of promiscuous relationships is not presented as an option.

Mindful of Mary Calderone's support for merging or reversing the sexes or sex roles and, in particular, 'abolishing the family as we know it', it is interesting to note what the FPA has to say on marriage in *Learning to Live with Sex*, its sex manual for 13- to 16-year-olds. The FPA explains that, while marriage as a formal commitment by two people to live together may be an ideal for individuals or society:

> Many marriages do not work out quite like that. More people are choosing to live together without formalising their vows because they may wish to separate later on, and some people are more tolerant of unfaithfulness or other close or sexual relationships outside of marriage.[37]

In 1977, the FPA and the Campaign for Homosexual Equality, with other sexual minority groups, organised a conference on

---

[36] *Love S.T.I.NGS*, FPA 1999

[37] *Learning to Live with Sex*, (revised edition) FPA, 1980.

'Sex Education: Where do we go from here?' The aim was to include material about sexual minority behaviour as a compulsory part of the school curriculum.[38]

The FPA's influence has been such that it is customary practice in Britain to demonstrate contraceptives to children in the classroom, with the message that they can be obtained from clinics where no one will inform their parents. Classroom quizzes and exam questions on contraceptives have also become part of the indoctrination process. As a spokesman stated on behalf of the FPA's Education Service in 1969: 'Contraceptive education has to be given very young, it is almost too late when the children get to puberty . . . children in school are a captive audience'.[39] It is hardly surprising, therefore, to read in the Monopolies Commission *Report on Contraceptive Sheaths* that London Rubber Industries submitted that the FPA's educational activities 'widen the market for contraceptives'.[40]

True to its aim to get at captive audiences in the classroom, in 1993 the FPA published *The Primary School Workbook* aimed at four- to eleven-year-olds. It is a perfect example of the way in which children can be indoctrinated, with sexual activity word puzzles and group activities for children in which seven year-olds can discuss masturbation. Teachers are told that 'sole and mutual masturbation is now encouraged as part of safer sex'. They are also told not to talk about marriage, but about the specialness of sexual relations. The main conclusion to be drawn from this unsavoury resource is that heterosexual marriage is

---

[38] *Sex Education – where do we go from here?* Conference leaflet, sponsored by The Albany Trust, Campaign for Homosexual Equality, Family Planning Association and the National Youth Bureau, 1977.

[39] Select Committee on Science and Technology (1969-70), *Minutes of Evidence on Population*, HMSO, 1970.

[40] *Contraceptive Sheaths, A Report on the Supply of Contraceptive Sheaths in the United Kingdom*, The Monopolies and Mergers Commission, HMSO, 1975.

merely one option among a range of sexual lifestyles from which to choose.[41]

Concern expressed to the Department for Education about this resource was summarily dismissed with the comment that it was produced by a long-established and well-respected agency and was much valued by teachers. The letter could have been written by the FPA itself – and possibly was! This is worrying because public education is a pursuit of the state and the sex education lobby support, above all else, an expansion of the scope of state intervention in the sex education of children.

In a graphically illustrated booklet aimed at boys aged 13-16, produced with funding from the Department of Health, the FPA discusses masturbation with approval, advising its readership that 'everyone' has 'fantasises while masturbating' and suggests that boys may be

> sexually interested in other men – or even men AND women. It's not a problem; your body is yours to share with whomever you choose.[42]

In a companion booklet, also funded by the Department of Health, identical messages are conveyed to girls aged 12–16.[43]

Contraception on Demand

There now appears to be no bottom age limit at which contraceptives can be supplied. A leaflet produced by the FPA for the Pharmacy Healthcare Scheme entitled *It doesn't matter how old you are* (1996) declares on its cover: 'Contraceptive advice and supplies are free to everyone', accompanied by an illustration of a birthday cake. The same message is conveyed in a guide to contraception for young people, aimed at 13–17-year-

---

[41] Gill Lenderyou, *Primary Schools Workbook, Teaching Sex Education within the National Curriculum*, Family Planning Association, 1993.

[42] *4Boys*, FPA 2000

[43] *4Girls*, FPA 2000

olds.[44] In response to the question: 'How old do I have to be [to get free information and help about contraception]?' the booklet states, 'Any age. It doesn't matter how old you are.' Young people are assured that their parents will not be informed: 'Even if you are under 16, doctors still have to keep everything you tell them private'. It is unlikely that a doctor or a nurse at a family planning clinic will refuse to give contraception to a young person under 16 because: 'The fact that you have asked for contraception shows that you have made a mature decision...' However, 'if a doctor does refuse to give you contraception you can ask why or try another doctor, family planning or young people's clinic, such as Brook.' Thus, the age of consent has been rendered an ineffective tool to protect girls from exploitation.

The FPA's attitude to parents is entirely consistent with Chisholm's view that they are suppressors of their children's better nature. Both the FPA and the Brook Advisory Centres advised the Department of Health on the memorandum on family planning services published in 1974, which removed parental responsibilities for their underage children. But even before that, the FPA advised adolescents to go to advisory clinics which will 'treat your problems sympathetically and not tell your parents unless you want them to know'.[45] The FPA and its offshoots bring all their power to bear upon parental moves to have their rights restored. The reason is clear. Lady Brook, founder and late president of the Brook Advisory Centres, wrote in reply to criticism of the sex education lobby:

> It is now the privilege of the Parental State to take major decisions – objective, unemotional, the State weighs up what is best for the child . . . [46]

---

[44] *Is everyone doing it? Your guide to contraception,* FPA 2000.

[45] *Learning to Live with Sex,* FPA, 1972.

[46] Letter to the Editor, *The Times,* 16 February 1980.

Chapter 4

Sex education: an ideological battleground

Few parents are aware of the extent to which sex education in schools has become an ideological battleground, on which a war is being waged for the hearts and minds of their children. For over half a century the IPPF and its member family planning associations have laboured to overcome children's natural modesty and the protective instincts of parents by means of compulsory sex education in schools linked to the provision of free birth control services without the knowledge or consent of parents.

The Parental Right of Withdrawal

In the political arena, one of the key issues to come to the fore has been whether sex education in schools should be mandatory for all pupils or whether parents should have the right to withdraw their children from classes which are contrary to their philosophical and religious beliefs, as is the case in religious education.

This debate has taken place amid growing controversy about the nature and effectiveness of sex education in schools over the past forty years. This controversy has occasioned a succession of amendments to Acts of Parliament and guidance documents from the Department for Education. These have addressed the question of whether and to what extent parents should have control over the provision of sex education in schools. The very suggestion that parents should be involved in determining the curriculum and the manner of its delivery has been vigorously opposed by the Family Planning Association, the Brook Advisory Centres and the Campaign for Homosexual Equality.

It was the 1993 Education Act which allowed parents for the first time to withdraw their children from all or part of the sex education programme (though not from science lessons covering human growth and reproduction) without needing to provide any explanation or to obtain permission from the school. It also gave parents a legal right to a copy of the school's sex education policy, a summary of which had to be included in the school prospectus. Parents were additionally entitled to a copy of any syllabus used by teachers and to see textbooks and other resources used in sex education.

This was followed by guidance from the Department of Education which stated that:

> Giving an individual pupil advice (on contraception) without parental knowledge or consent would be an inappropriate exercise of a teacher's responsibilities.[47]

The following year the government was heavily criticised by the United Nations Committee on the Rights of the Child which viewed the parental right of withdrawal as a breach of the right of the child to express his/her opinion.[48]

The Children's Legal Centre, which was established in 1981 in the aftermath of the 1979 International Year of the Child, considered it 'irresponsible' to allow parents the freedom to withdraw their children from sex education classes and was 'appalled' that parents would wish to deprive their children of such instruction on the grounds of immorality.[49]

The Children's Rights Development Unit (CRDU) was similarly 'disturbed' by the thought of parents being able to control and veto the sex education received by their children in

---

[47] Department for Education (1994) *Sex Education in Schools*. Circular 5/94, London: HMSO.

[48] Concluding observations of the Committee on the Rights of the Child: United Kingdom of Great Britain and Northern Ireland. 15/02/95. CRC/C/15/Add.34

[49] *Childright*, Issue 98, July 1993

school. In its *UK Agenda for Children*, it asserted that basic information about human development and reproduction is insufficient. Children needed family planning education - and they needed it 'from a very early age'. The *Agenda* insisted that in order to comply with the UN Convention on the Rights of the Child:

> Sex education in school, linked to the National Curriculum, should be available to all children and young people, and taught at an age when it will be of use to them and in a manner sensitive to their needs. Governors should not be responsible for deciding whether or not a school provides sex education. There should be special training for staff involved and parents should not have the right to withdraw their children. If parental right of withdrawal from sex education stands, then at the very least arrangements should be made to monitor the numbers and reasons for such withdrawal with a view to reviewing the provision.[50]

However, notwithstanding intense pressure from children's rights activists and international monitoring bodies, the parental right of withdrawal from sex education classes remained in place and was restated in the Education Act 1996. The Act also required governing bodies to make the school's written policy on sex and relationships education (SRE) available to parents. This policy was to include information on how and by whom SRE is provided, together with details of how it is monitored and evaluated.

The national curriculum requires that:

> Secondary schools must provide sex education for their pupils. It must include teaching about AIDS, HIV and other sexually transmitted infections and be given in such a way as to encourage pupils to have due regard to

---

[50] Gerison Lansdown and Peter Newell, *UK agenda for children*. London: CRDU, 1994, p.106.

34

moral considerations and the value of family life. The detailed content and nature of sex education is for schools to decide. Parents can choose to withdraw their children from all or part of sex education.[51]

Primary school governing bodies, however, are free to decide whether or not to include SRE within their school's curriculum (with the exception of aspects of reproduction taught in science). A written note of their decision must be kept on record, and if they do opt to provide SRE, the schools are responsible for determining how it is organised.

In July 2000, the DfEE issued fresh guidance on Sex and Relationship Education to replace Circular 5/94, taking account of the revised national curriculum.[52] The document displays an ambivalence towards marriage. While the guidance states that 'pupils should be taught about the nature and importance of marriage for family life and bringing up children', it stresses that, since 'there are strong and mutually supportive relationships outside marriage . . . , pupils should learn the significance of marriage and stable relationships as key building blocks of community and society'. It goes on to add that, 'Care needs to be taken to ensure that there is no stigmatisation of children based on their home circumstances'. Throughout the document there is an emphasis on the need to involve parents in developing and reviewing the school's policy, and caution is expressed regarding the types of material used.

While the law has continued to insist that schools 'have due regard to moral considerations and the value of family life' in the delivery of sex education, neither 'moral considerations' nor 'family life' are defined, and the way they are interpreted becomes more elastic as time goes on. According to an FPA guide, the moral framework for sex education should not be

---

[51] National Curriculum Online http://www.nc.uk.net/notes_34.html

[52] Department for Education and Employment (2000), *Sex and Relationship Education Guidance*, Circular 0116/2000.

'made up of a single set of prescriptive values' which would 'exclude pupils who fail to adhere to these values or who choose not to conform'. Rather, teachers and governors are encouraged to develop 'a set of core values which are inclusive of all young people and of the adults who work with them'.[53] It would be difficult to conceive of a more effective way of robbing the term 'moral considerations' of any meaning at all.

As with the DfEE in its attitude towards marriage, what the FPA gives with one hand, it takes away with the other. While it pays lip service to 'respecting religious and cultural identities' in sex education, it is far more enthusiastic about 'refusing to tolerate prejudice', 'learning to respect diversity', and 'recognising, respecting and celebrating difference so that no one is excluded',[54] apparently oblivious to the fact that a prior commitment to an inclusivist approach will inevitably undermine the moral stance of many faith groups.

Although legislation and guidance gives considerable discretion to schools in the content of sex education, in practice schools are bombarded with sex education materials from bodies whose understanding of moral considerations and family life would be far removed from that of the majority of parents. Although schools are encouraged to involve parents in developing sex education policies, it requires constant vigilance and considerable determination to oppose curriculum resources prepared or promoted by publicly-funded bodies.

Section 28

Throughout the 1980s, concerns were expressed about the way in which many local authorities were vigorously promoting homosexuality by means of equal opportunities policies,

---

[53] Gill Mullinar, *Developing sex education in schools: a practical guide*, Family Planning Association 1994, p.39.

[54] *Ibid.*, p.13, 39

sponsoring events designed for homosexuals and running courses on 'challenging heterosexism'. Books on gay and lesbian themes were promoted through public libraries, and local education authorities, particularly in the London area, were beginning to encourage teaching about homosexuality in schools. For example, headteachers in Haringey were advised that it was now the council's education policy 'to promote positive images of lesbians and gays – from nursery through to further education'. Similarly, Ealing Council resolved to 'promote positive attitudes to homosexuality, removing any sexist or heterosexual practices and materials'.[55]

In response to the widespread public disquiet surrounding these developments, the Local Government Act 1988 included the now infamous 'Section 28' which required that a local authority shall not

a) intentionally promote homosexuality or publish material with the intention of promoting homo-sexuality;

b) promote the teaching in any maintained school of the acceptability of homosexuality as a pretended family relationship.

While Section 28 led some local authorities to review their education policies, a legal opinion given to the Association of London Authorities and the National Council for Civil Liberties set out to show how local authorities may promote homosexuality while remaining within the law. The legal opinion reasoned that Section 28 only prohibited direct advocacy to individuals to engage in homosexual activities. Several years later, the Department for Education and Employment issued guidance in which it observed that while Section 28 applied to local education authorities, it did not apply

---

[55] Rachel Tingle, *The Ideology and Politics of the Gay Movement.* http://www.trushare.com/29OCT97/imptingl.txt

directly to schools, implying that so long as the local education authority was not involved, schools were free to promote homosexuality.[56]

Nevertheless, opposition to the clause continued unabated. Children's rights campaigners joined forces with homosexual activists and the 'sex education establishment' to call for the repeal of Section 28 on the basis that it breached the child's 'right to know' about different forms of sexual expression and that it denied them 'the right to express their own homosexuality'. In its submission to the United Nations Committee on the Rights of the Child, the Children's Rights Development Unit complained that:

> The restrictive nature of this legislation and its explicit denial of the validity of homosexual relationships may mean that children are denied the opportunity to understand and learn about different expressions of sexuality. They may also be effectively denied the right to express their own homosexuality and to discuss it with sympathetic adults who might be able to help them come to terms with the choices available to them and affirm the legitimacy of their sexuality.[57]

Given that the age of consent for homosexuals stood at 21 when this was written and that the subjects of concern to the CRDU were schoolchildren aged under 16, it would appear that there is a broader agenda at work than simply the promotion of positive images of homosexuality.

Although Section 28 undoubtedly had a restraining effect on the content of sex education in schools in many parts of England and Wales, it did not entirely eliminate the use of materials presenting positive images of homosexual activity. There are now justifiable fears that in the absence of any

---

[56] Department for Education (1994) *Sex Education in Schools.* Circular 5/94, London: HMSO.

[57] Lansdown and Newell, *op cit.*, p10

restraining legislation or alternative safeguards, the repeal of Section 28 under the Local Government Act 2003, will send the signal to sex educators that it is permissible to promote homosexuality in schools.

Chapter 5

The teenage pregnancy strategy

Among the first initiatives of Tony Blair following his rise to power in 1997 was the establishment of the Social Exclusion Unit (SEU). The unit's remit is to help improve Government action to reduce social exclusion in England by producing 'joined-up solutions to joined-up problems'. Amidst growing concerns at Britain having the highest rate of teenage pregnancies in Western Europe, the SEU was commissioned to undertake a major study into the reasons for this and to 'develop an integrated strategy to cut rates of teenage parenthood, particularly underage parenthood, towards the European average, and propose better solutions to combat the risk of social exclusion for vulnerable teenage parents and their children'.[58]

Teenage Pregnancy Report

The ensuing report, *Teenage Pregnancy*, published in 1999, acknowledged the scale of the problem and its social consequences. In his introduction, the Prime Minister wrote:

> Teenage mothers are less likely to finish their education, less likely to find a good job, and more likely to end up both as single parents and bringing up their children in poverty. The children themselves run a much greater risk of poor health, and have a much higher chance of becoming teenage mothers themselves. Our failure to tackle this problem has cost the teenagers, their children and the country dear.

---

[58] Social Exclusion Unit, *Teenage Pregnancy*, London: HMSO, 1999, p.2.

40

The report committed the government to two main goals:

- Reducing the rate of teenage conceptions, with the specific aim of halving the rate of conceptions among under-18s by 2010 [and]
- Getting more teenage parents into education, training or employment, to reduce their risk of long-term social exclusion.

An action plan was proposed, with an emphasis on 'better education' combined with free availability of contraception to young people in an attempt to meet the first target, and 'better support' for teenage mothers in an attempt to meet the second. Nowhere does the report allow for the possibility that the two goals may be mutually exclusive, in that the deployment of resources to provide improved housing, educational opportunities, employment training and access to childcare may result in an incentive to teenage motherhood to those caught in the 'cycle of despair' to which the Prime Minister refers.[59]

Neither does the report acknowledge that just seven years previously in 1992, a government white paper, *The Health of the Nation: A Strategy for Health in England*, had set a similar target to:

> reduce the rate of conceptions amongst the under-16s by at least 50% by the year 2000 (from 9.5 per 1,000 girls aged 13–15 in 1989 to no more than 4.8).[60]

In view of the fact that the government dismally failed to meet its target, with the under-16 conception rate standing at 8.3 per thousand in 2000, one might have expected at least some analysis of the earlier strategy and discussion of possible reasons for its failure. In fact, this was not the first time that an approach dependent on sex education and contraception had failed to

---

[59] *Ibid*, p.4

[60] *The Health of the Nation: A strategy for health in England*, Cm1986, London HMSO, p.95

deliver. In 1976 the FPA set itself the target of halving the number of unwanted pregnancies by 1986. The target featured in the association's annual reports until 1981/82 after which it was conveniently forgotten. Never prepared to concede defeat, the FPA's 1987/88 annual report stated:

> In recent years there has been much talk within and around the FPA of the organisation having achieved its aims and needing new ones.[61]

Nevertheless, the *Teenage Pregnancy* report stubbornly persists with a dogged reliance on sex education and contraceptive services to reduce the teenage pregnancy rate.

Teenage Pregnancy Unit

As part of its current teenage pregnancy strategy, the government has established the Teenage Pregnancy Unit (TPU) as a cross-government unit, originally based within the Department of Health but now located in the Department for Education and Skills under the oversight of the minister for children. The TPU has been charged with implementing the strategy, assisted by the Independent Advisory Group on Teenage Pregnancy (IAG) whose role is to advise the government and monitor the success of the strategy. Alison Hadley, the TPU programme manager, joined the Unit after 13 years with Brook, where she served as national policy officer. In her current role she is responsible for policy on 'contraception and advice services for young people, including confidentiality, emergency contraception, and abortion' and serves as policy lead for 'supporting parents'. It is therefore perhaps not surprising to find on the home page of the TPU website that teenagers, young people and their parents are directed to the Brook website 'for advice on sexual health or pregnancy issues'.

---

[61] Family Planning Association, Annual Report 1987/88, p.4

The Independent Advisory Group on Teenage Pregnancy is similarly formed of individuals who are wedded to a failed methodology. For example, Gill Frances (who has also written under the name of Gill Lenderyou), deputy chair of the IAG, wrote the *Primary School Workbook* (see p. 29) while training and development officer for the FPA and chair of London Brook Advisory Centres. She is currently director of children's development at the National Children's Bureau (NCB), having previously served as director of the Sex Education Forum (SEF) which is housed in the same building. The intense cross-linking in the IAG of individuals representing a narrow spectrum of opinion raises questions about the true 'independence' of the Group.[62] The Group contains no representatives of organisations representing the traditional family based on marriage, nor of groups advocating abstinence as a means of reducing teenage pregnancy. Nor has the Teenage Pregnancy Unit at any stage sought input from such groups. Even at a local level there is some evidence that only those who were likely to be sympathetic towards the approach being adopted were consulted

---

[62] Other members of the IAG include Jan Barlow, chief executive of Brook; Simon Blake, who currently assists Gill Frances at the NCB, having also previously been director of the SEF and worked for the FPA; Kate Davies, who managed the Brixton Brook advisory centre during the late 1980s; Jane Fraser who worked for Brook for over 30 years; Rachel Garbutt, who is a previous director of Brook Manchester; and Anne Weyman, who is chief executive of the FPA, having previously worked for the NCB where she founded the SEF of which she is currently the president. In addition, Roger Ingham of the Centre for Sexual Health Research at the University of Southampton has been closely associated with Brook over a number of years: in 1997 he was awarded a Department of Health grant to work on a research project in conjunction with Brook; in 1998, he addressed the Brook annual conference; and in 1999 was commissioned by Brook to conduct a study funded by the Department of Health. Another member of the IAG, Dilys Went, has worked in association with the education and publication units of both Brook and FPA, and Hansa Patel-Kanwal co-authored a training guide jointly produced by the FPA and NCB and funded by the Teenage Pregnancy Unit.

and that those taking a different view were excluded from the consultation process.[63]

Notwithstanding the poor track record of attempts to reduce teenage pregnancy rates by means of sex education and easier access to contraception, with the wheels already set in motion, the bandwagon continues to roll, now bearing the imprimatur of the TPU and the IAG as well as the sex education and family planning establishment, with all its vested interests. The DfEE guidance on sex and relationship education (SRE), published in 2000, accordingly emphasises the priority of contraceptive education in schools:

> Trained staff in secondary schools should be able to give young people full information about different types of contraception, including emergency contraception, and their effectiveness... Trained teachers can also give pupils – individually and as a class – additional information and guidance on where they can obtain confidential advice, counselling and, where necessary, treatment.[64]

Ignorance is not the Problem

However, the DfEE is labouring under the common mis-apprehension that sex education is effective in delaying sexual activity:

> Research demonstrates that good, comprehensive sex and relationship education does not make young people more likely to enter into sexual activity. Indeed it can help them learn the reasons for, and the benefits to be gained from, delaying such activity.[65]

---

[63] *Why the Government's Teenage Pregnancy Strategy is destined to fail*, London: Family Education Trust 2002, p.12.

[64] *Ibid*, para 2.11

[65] *Ibid.*, para 1.7

In reality, however, while there is evidence that sex education programmes provide contraceptive *knowledge* and may result in changes in *attitude* on the part of young people, evidence that it affects subsequent sexual *behaviour* is lacking. In June 2002 the *British Medical Journal* carried two articles which raised questions about the extent to which sex education can be expected to reduce teenage pregnancy rates.

The first of these studies focussed on 8,430 pupils aged between 13 and 15 in the Tayside and Lothian regions of Scotland who participated in a programme called SHARE (Sexual Health & Relationships: Safe, Happy and Responsible), designed to reduce unsafe sexual practices. It was an elaborate and well-resourced showpiece programme, involving the training of 80 teachers and delivered over two years of the curriculum, with a follow-up of the participants two years later. Young people in the control group received more conventional sex education. The follow-up revealed that the programme had made no impact. Those who participated were not less likely to have become sexually active or to have practised 'unsafe sex'.[66]

The second study reviewed the effectiveness of sex education in delaying sexual intercourse, improving the use of birth control and reducing unwanted pregnancies by examining the best research available. After eliminating studies which were methodologically weak, the authors concentrated on 26 randomised controlled trials described in 22 reports, all in the USA. The conclusion was that the programmes 'did not delay the initiation of sexual intercourse in young women or young men; did not improve use of birth control by young women at every intercourse or at last intercourse or by young men at every

---

[66] D. Wight *et al.*, 'Limits of teacher delivered sex education: interim behavioural outcomes from randomised trial', *British Medical Journal*, Vol. 324, 15 June 2002.

intercourse or at last intercourse; and did not reduce pregnancy rates in young women'.[67]

There is also a lack of evidence to demonstrate that contraceptive availability to young people is effective in reducing the rate of teenage conceptions. This is reflected in the numbers of young people attending family planning clinics in England. While attendances by girls under the age of 16 increased almost fourfold from 18,000 in 1989 to 68,000 in 1999, this rise was not matched by any reduction in teenage conception rates which remained more or less constant throughout the period.

A study published in the *British Medical Journal* found that of 240 teenagers who became pregnant, 93% had seen a health professional at least once during the previous year, and 71% had specifically discussed contraception. The researchers concluded that:

- Most teenagers who become pregnant do consult their GP during the year before pregnancy, suggesting that potential barriers to care are less than often supposed.

- Teenagers who become pregnant are more likely to have consulted their GP during the year prior to conception than other teenagers, and most of the difference is owing to consultation for contraception.

- Teenagers who have an abortion are more likely to have received emergency contraception.[68]

A survey of over 2,000 young people aged 13-15 found that, of those who were sexually active, two-thirds said that their first sexual relationship had not been the result of conscious

---

[67] A. DiCenso *et al.*, 'Interventions to reduce unintended pregnancies among adolescents: systematic review of randomised controlled trials', *British Medical Journal*, Vol. 324, 15 June 2002.

[68] D Churchill, J Allen, M Pringle, J Hippisley-Cox, D Ebdon, M Macpherson *et al.* 'Consultation patterns and provision of contraception in general practice before teenage pregnancy', *BMJ* 2000; 321:486-489.

decision-making. For 30% 'it just happened'; 19% were drunk; 6% were talked into it by their partners; 3% cited peer pressure; and a worrying 4% (all girls) said they had no choice.[69]

All in all, the evidence suggests that the government's teenage pregnancy strategy rests on a false premise. Ignorance is not the problem; therefore we cannot hope to solve it by means of sex education and contraceptive provision. Not only is this well-worn approach ineffective, but there is also evidence to suggest that it is counter-productive and merely exacerbates the problem.

A study undertaken by Dr David Paton and published in the peer-reviewed *Journal of Health Economics* examined whether improved access to family planning services for under-16s is likely to contribute to a reduction in underage conceptions. Drawing on official figures, Dr Paton considered the impact of a Court of Appeal ruling in December 1984 which had prevented health professionals from providing contraceptives to females under the age of 16 without the consent of their parents. Until it was overturned in the House of Lords in the autumn of the following year, the ruling had the effect of significantly reducing the number of underage girls attending family planning clinics to seek contraceptive advice. However, contrary to forecasts, Dr Paton found no corresponding increase in underage conceptions during the period. Rather, he concluded that while improved access to contraception reduces the risk of pregnancy, at the same time it raises the likelihood of engaging in sexual activity in the first place, resulting in an overall increase in conceptions to young women under the age of 16.[70]

---

[69] C Hill, *Sex Under Sixteen?* London: Family Education Trust, 2000.

[70] D Paton (2002) 'The Economics of Family Planning and Underage Conceptions', *Journal of Health Economics*, 21, 2 (March), 27-45

Local Teenage Pregnancy Strategies

As part of the government's commitment to 'joined-up action', the Teenage Pregnancy Unit was charged with responsibility for ensuring that local authorities and health authorities throughout England jointly identified a teenage pregnancy co-ordinator, whose primary role would be to serve as 'local champions for action and services to prevent teenage pregnancy and support teenage parents, and lead the process of local co-ordination working through Health Improvement Programmes'.[71] Using guidance produced by the TPU, all local authorities and regional health authorities were required to produce a teenage pregnancy strategy with 'exciting' and 'innovative' ideas about how they could contribute to meeting the government's targets by 2010. A survey of a sample of these local strategies drawn from different parts of the country found that far from containing initiatives that could remotely be described as 'exciting' or 'innovative', there is a uniform reliance on 'better' and 'earlier' sex education and contraceptive provision, amounting to little more than a rebranding of approaches that have been tried and found wanting.[72]

Indeed, several of the strategy documents appear to lose sight of their original remit in their enthusiasm to facilitate young people's sexual relationships. For example, the 'strategic vision' of East Kent is that 'children and young people' should 'be aware of and enjoy their sexuality'. Similarly, the Essex strategy 'is designed to... provide appropriate advice and support for young people in their physical, emotional and moral development as they begin to explore their own sexuality and become sexually active'. The Swindon strategy promises that 'community responsibility and positive attitudes towards sex and relationships in young people will be fostered across

---

[71] http://www.teenagepregnancyunit.gov.uk/

[72] *Why the Government's Teenage Pregnancy Strategy is Destined to Fail*, London: Family Education Trust 2002

Swindon' and takes the view that, 'Young people have the right to freedom from disease' and that 'Young women have the right to freedom from unplanned pregnancy and a fulfilling sex life'.[73]

Given the make-up of the TPU and its advisory group, and the presuppositions on which their work is based, they are unlikely to contribute to reducing the teenage sexual activity that gives rise to teenage conceptions. While the vigorous promotion of the 'morning-after pill' may be able to mask the teenage conception rate, it will not be able to arrest the alarming upward trend in rates of STI infection among young people.

The Crisis in Sexual Health

In England, Wales and Northern Ireland there was a 74% increase in cases of gonorrhoea in girls under 16 between 1995 and 2000, and a 107% rise in diagnoses of chlamydia in underage girls over the same period. In an editorial in the journal *Sexually Transmitted Infections*, published in April 2003, Professor Michael Adler of the Royal Free and University College Medical School, who headed up the government's HIV/AIDS and Sexual Health Strategy, observed that England had missed almost every one of the sexual health targets set out in the 1992 report *Health of the Nation* and that, in most instances, sexual health had declined. He concluded that it is 'no exaggeration that we now face a public health crisis in relation to sexual health'.[74]

Two months later, the House of Commons Health Select Committee also used the word 'crisis' when publishing findings from its Sexual Health Inquiry. The Committee's report concluded:

> We have been appalled by the crisis in sexual health we have heard about and witnessed during our inquiry. We

---

[73] *Ibid.*, p.9

[74] M Adler, 'Sexual health—health of the nation' *Sex Transm Infect.*2003; 79: 85-87

do not use the word 'crisis' lightly but in this case it is appropriate. This is a major public health issue and the problems identified in this Report must be addressed immediately.[75]

The Health Committee commented that no area of public health in England had suffered a more dramatic and widespread decline in recent years than sexual health and noted that 42% of females with gonorrhoea and 36% of females with genital chlamydial infection were under 20 years of age, and that among 12- to 15-year-old females diagnosed with gonorrhoea, almost a quarter would return with another episode of the disease within a year.[76]

Yet, in spite of the government's failure to meet its *Health of the Nation* targets, the Committee proposed to address the current crisis with more of the same and 'strongly recommend[ed] that SRE becomes a core part of the National Curriculum, to be delivered within the broader framework of PSHE along with citizenship'.[77]

The Committee also called on the government to 'explore the possibility of improving young people's access to health services through providing specialist advice facilities',[78] even though such government-funded initiatives had failed even to arrest, let alone reverse, the decline in sexual health.

The main weapon being deployed by the government in its war against teenage pregnancy and STIs is the condom, and vast sums of money have been invested to promote condom usage under the banner of 'safer sex' campaigns. Yet the limitations of condoms for reducing conception rates and for protecting against STIs receive little attention in campaign literature. With

---

[75] House of Commons Health Committee, *Sexual Health*, Third Report of Session 2002-03 Vol 1, p.94

[76] *Ibid.*, p.7, 9

[77] *Ibid.*, p.83

[78] *Ibid.*, p.6

a method failure rate of 3% and a user failure rate as high as 14%, one in seven sexually active women will become pregnant each year notwithstanding condom use. Since young people are less efficient users of condoms than those with more experience, the risk for them is even greater. However, as Dr Trevor Stammers has noted:

> Contraceptive failure rates are calculated only in relation to resulting pregnancies. The risk of STI transmission is much higher, as pregnancy only occurs during the fertile phase of the menstrual cycle, whereas STIs can be transmitted throughout the cycle.[79]

While a report from the US Department of Health and Human Services concluded that consistent condom use is 85% effective in reducing the risk of HIV transmission and provides protection against gonorrhoea, it also noted there is no conclusive evidence that the use of condoms substantially reduces the transmission of human papilloma virus, genital herpes or chlamydia.[80]

There is additionally the question of whether condom usage may lull users into a false sense of security and contribute to an increase in promiscuous behaviour, carrying with it a higher risk of infection. An article in the *Lancet* highlighted parallels between the rise in the number of road deaths that followed the introduction of legislation requiring the use of seat-belts and the increase in the incidence of STIs following vigorous campaigns to promote condoms.[81]

As Dr Stammers comments:

> The theoretical protection offered by condom use in a sexually active population as a whole may be cancelled out in practice by other changes in sexual behaviour.

---

[79] T Stammers, *The Condom Controversy*, London: Family Education Trust 2002.

[80] www.niaid.nih.gov/dmid/stds/condomreport.pdf

[81] J Richens, J Imrie, A Copas, 'Condoms and seat belts: the parallels and the lessons', *Lancet* 2000; 355:400-403.

This principle of *risk displacement* is well-recognised in many areas of public health. It explains why, for example, the numbers of road traffic accident deaths have not decreased in the UK despite the introduction of seat belt laws. Belted drivers tend to drive faster than they did before and, consequently, more pedestrians and cyclists are killed. In a similar way, over-confidence in the 'safety' of condoms easily leads to an increased frequency of sexual intercourse with either the same partner or a number of other partners. Given the 14% condom failure rate, this means that condom promotion, without addressing such consequent changes in sexual behaviour, will inevitably result in an increase in STI transmission and unplanned conceptions, such as we have seen in the UK.[82]

---

[82] T Stammers, *The Condom Controversy*, London: Family Education Trust 2002.

Chapter 6

Saying no to abstinence

Since its formation in 1987 under the directorship of Anne Weyman (now chief executive of the FPA) the Sex Education Forum (SEF), based within the National Children's Bureau, has become extremely influential in the development of sex education in schools. An umbrella organisation, consisting of 50 organisations with an interest in the field, SEF describes itself as 'the national authority on sex and relationships education (SRE)'. It believes that 'good quality SRE is an entitlement for all children and young people'.[83] Forum members include Brook, FPA, Families and Friends of Lesbians and Gays, the Health Education Authority, Lesbian and Gay Christian Movement, and the Terrence Higgins Trust, as well as heavyweights like Barnardos and the NSPCC.

The SEF is in receipt of public funds from both the Department for Education and the Department of Health. It has also developed close links with the Teenage Pregnancy Unit which was established by the government in 1999, ostensibly to reduce the high incidence of teenage pregnancies in the UK. In addition to the presence of three previous directors of the Forum on its Independent Advisory Group, the TPU has funded various SEF projects. The TPU clearly regards the SEF as the central point of reference for teachers of sex and relationships education seeking to identify suitable materials for use with young people.

The SEF professes to draw on 'the best existing practices to identify positive strategies and approaches'. However, its mind is emphatically closed to the possibility that abstinence education might be effective in reducing the teenage sexual

---

[83] http://www.ncb.org.uk/sef/

activity that leads to teenage conceptions and sexually transmitted infections. In 2001 it published a booklet entitled *Just Say No! to Abstinence Education,* based on a sex education study tour of the United States by Simon Blake and Gill Frances. The authors spoke with sixteen individuals or organisations interested in sex education in the USA of which only three could be described as advocates of abstinence-only education. In their report, they lump together many programmes of varied quality and focus on the weakest as if they are representative of all the programmes available. The Teenage Pregnancy Unit has received the report favourably and carries a link to a summary sheet of the study on its website.

Although the SEF has never been inhibited from promoting its own favoured approach to sex education despite a lack of supporting evidence, when it comes to abstinence education there is an insistence on the need for rigorous research. This dual standard is common amongst the advocates of sex education. Contraceptive education has been provided in schools for several decades in the absence of any evidence of its effectiveness, while impossibly high standards of proof of effectiveness are being demanded for abstinence education, which is only a few years old.

In a communication to all doctors in January 2003, the Chief Medical Officer (CMO) Sir Liam Donaldson went out of his way to state that: 'Evidence does not exist to suggest that abstinence approaches are effective in sex education.' On the other hand, he asserted that there was 'strong evidence for the effectiveness of sex and relationships education, when linked to contraceptive services'.[84]

In common with the SEF and the TPU, the CMO vastly overestimates the impact of contraceptive education and provision while ignoring the positive potential of an abstinence-

---

[84] Sir Liam Donaldson, *CMO's Update 35,* January 2003 www.doh.gov.uk/cmo/cmo_35.html#10.

based approach. While it is true that more research into abstinence education is required to assess the extent of its impact on teenage sexual activity in the United States, preliminary studies, backed by the fact that teenage pregnancy rates in the US declined by 19% from 1991 to 1997, suggest that it has had at least some positive effect on teenagers' attitudes and behaviour.[85] Even if they feel that it is too early to pronounce on the effectiveness of abstinence programmes, given the failure of the contraceptive-based approach over three decades, one might have thought that the SEF, TPU and CMO might at least be prepared to find a place for abstinence education among their 'promising approaches' in view of the emerging evidence from the USA. However, such is their ideological hostility to the idea, that there is a strong resistance to giving it any serious consideration.

Sex education in the Netherlands

In support of their reliance on 'better' sex education coupled with contraceptive services to reduce teenage pregnancy rates, the Netherlands is frequently held up by the SEF and its affiliates as a model worthy of emulation. In 2000, conception rates in the Netherlands stood at 14.1 per 1,000 young women aged 15-19, while in England and Wales they were over four times higher at 62.2 per 1,000.[86] It is claimed that a major factor behind the lower rates in the Netherlands is:

> an earlier and more open approach to sexual issues in schools and in families. This is associated...with greater levels of discussion and forward planning between partners, later ages at first sexual intercourse, more

---

[85] *Trends in Pregnancy Rates for the United States, 1976-97: An Update.* NVSR 49, No. 4. 10 pp. (PHS) 6 June 2001.

[86] ONS (2002) *Population Trends* 109; J Rademakers (2002) *Abortus in Nederland*, Heemstede: STISAN; CBS (2001) Samenleven: Nieue Feiten

effective contraceptive use, and lower levels of subsequent regret.[87]

A booklet commissioned by the TPU and published by the SEF similarly attributes lower teenage pregnancy rates in the Netherlands to a 'culture of openness' about sexual matters:

> In countries such as Sweden and the Netherlands, young people grow up in a culture which is open and honest about sexual matters, and supportive of their developing sexuality. This enables young people to develop a sense of pride in their bodies rather than overwhelming feelings of anxiety, confusion and embarrassment.[88]

The SEF believes that sex education holds the key to reproducing such a culture in the UK, and breaking down inhibitions. In a factsheet on *Meeting the needs of girls and young women in sex and relationships education*, it advocates small mixed gender groups as the most effective way to overcome reticence and achieve a more honest and open exchange of opinions and views.[89]

However, a recent study of sex education in the Netherlands suggests that there is no discernible uniform approach to sex education in the Netherlands that would permit a direct correlation to be drawn between sex education provision and teenage conception rates. Rather, there is a high degree of autonomy in curriculum development and policy-making, considerable diversity in terms of content and teaching style, and stronger influence from parents and churches. The research found that Dutch sex education is not as 'open' and permissive as is often claimed, but is delivered within a firm moral

---

[87] Roger Ingham, 'Doctors should advise adolescents to abstain from sex: against', *British Medical Journal* vol 321 (16 December 2000): 1522.

[88] Sarah Thistle, *Secondary schools and sexual health services: Forging the links*, Sex Education Forum 2003, p.2

[89] Forum Factsheet 21, *Meeting the needs of girls and young women in sex and relationships education*, Sex Education Forum 2000.

framework. Indeed, as in the UK, sexual health experts in the Netherlands have expressed concern that an emphasis on setting the expression of sexuality within the context of committed enduring relationships is too restrictive when teenagers may want to experiment with sexual activity.[90]

The same study also found a lack of evidence to support the assertion that the rate of teenage conceptions in the Netherlands has been reduced by means of the easy availability of contraception to young people. In what has been described as 'an almost perfect contraceptive population' where condom use rose among the sexually active from 17% in 1981 to 85% in 1994,[91] there has been no corresponding reduction in the rates of either teenage pregnancies or abortions, and there are early signs of an overall rise in the rate of STI-incidence, particularly of chlamydia which affects young people disproportionately.[92] Equally important is the finding that, during the 1990s, the abortion rate rose despite a widespread increase in contraceptive use.[93]

It is therefore apparent that the lower teenage conception rate in the Netherlands cannot be attributed to a simple combination of sex education, an 'open culture' and widespread contraceptive use. Rather, it is necessary to take into account a more complex set of cultural factors besides which sex education, of whatever quality, is insignificant. There is now a considerable volume of research which identifies factors known to influence the likelihood of young people becoming sexually

---

[90] Joost van Loon, *Deconstructing the Dutch Utopia: Sex education and teenage pregnancy in the Netherlands*, London: Family Education Trust 2003.

[91] E Ketting. and A P Visser (1994) 'Contraception in the Netherlands: the low abortion rate explained'. *Patient Education and Counselling*, 23:161-171.

[92] M J W van der Laar, K Haks, and T Coenen (2002) 'Sterke stijging SOA in 2001' [Strong increase of STIs in 2001]. *Infectieziekten Bulletin* 13 (8): 293–296.

[93] CBS (2001) *Samenleven: Nieue Feiten over Relaties en Gezinnen* [Living Together: New Facts about Relationships and Families] Voorburg: Centraal Bureau voor de Statistiek.

active. Most important among these is the link between the breakdown of the family based on marriage and premature sexual experimentation. While Dutch family law is noted for its liberal character, patterns of family life in the Netherlands have generally remained more traditional than in many other Northern and Western European countries. Compared with the UK, the Netherlands has a far lower proportion of lone-parent families, out-of-wedlock births, divorces and mothers in full-time employment. Combined with lower welfare benefits to teenage mothers and the persistence of stigma, these structural differences offer a far more convincing explanation for the differing teenage conception rates.[94]

Damage Limitation

The government's teenage pregnancy strategy, with the full support of the Sex Education Forum and its member organisations including Brook and the FPA, is based on the premise that it is unrealistic to expect young people to abstain from sexual activity. They have therefore chosen to embark on a damage limitation exercise dependent on condom usage to reduce the risk of pregnancy and of contracting some STIs, and on the use of the morning-after pill as a back-up when all else fails. The truth is, however, that the vast majority of young people under the age of 16 are not engaged in sexual relationships. A national survey of 2,250 students aged 13-15 found that only 17% claimed to be sexually active.[95] It might therefore be a wiser course of action to support and affirm the majority in their abstinence, and to demonstrate to the minority the physical, emotional and psychological benefits of delaying sexual activity until marriage, where it serves as an expression of the total self-giving of the one to the other which lies at the heart of a lifelong commitment. Until our sex educators

---

[94] Joost van Loon, *op cit.*

[95] C Hill, *op cit.*

overcome their phobia about abstinence and their obsession with sexual expression, they are unlikely to make any positive progress.

Chapter 7

The elimination of parents

Of all the 'reforms' achieved by the Family Planning Association and its network, the most insidious has surely been the provision of contraceptives to underage children without the knowledge or consent of their parents. It can be no coincidence that Chisholm's 'elimination of the ways of the elders' has taken place in a number of countries. Indeed, there is pressure worldwide to minimise the requirement for 'third-party consent'.[96]

In Britain, by a process which can be described as 'the inevitability of gradualism', the state has taken over from parents. In the 1960s, arguments were put forward by the FPA that making contraception available to the unmarried would reduce out-of-wedlock pregnancies, an argument subsequently taken up by the abortion law reformers. On the contrary, rising figures of out-of-wedlock pregnancies and abortions followed the easy availability of contraception and abortion. The propaganda line changed to the need for a *free* contraceptive service to reduce the number of abortions. This pressure culminated in the passing of the National Health (Reorganisation) Act (1973) which mandated birth control services for all, including children.

Following the passage of this Act, an advisory memorandum on family planning services was issued by the Department of Health in 1974.[97] This *diktat* included a section on the young with advice from the Medical Defence Union that

---

[96] *The Use of Para-Medicals for Primary Health Care in the Commonwealth,* Commonwealth Secretariat, 1979.

[97] *Family Planning Services,* Memorandum of Guidance, Department of Health and Social Security, May 1974.

the parents of a child of whatever age should not be contacted without the child's permission. This was at complete variance with medical practice at the time in all other areas of treatment of underage children. For parents it was, and remains, an impossible situation. They are held responsible for the behaviour of their children, and must pay any fines incurred by them, but they are not to be told when their daughters are the subjects of unlawful acts. The Department of Health's *diktat* also had the effect of virtually nullifying the age of consent law without reference to Parliament, and it did so at a time when the paedophile movement was seeking its abolition, or its reduction to four years of age.

Despite repeated efforts to reverse the Department of Health's policy employing every democratic means possible, including Mrs Victoria Gillick's private legal action to have the memorandum declared illegal, the overwhelming will of the public on this issue has been ignored by the bureaucracy. Children have the ultimate right to refuse to allow doctors and professionals to consult their parents.

The IPPF has made its position on this matter absolutely clear. In the report *The Human Right to Family Planning* it claims, under the heading 'Rights of Young People', that the 'adolescent age group (10-19 years)' should have full access to fertility regulation, information and services, with guaranteed privacy and confidentiality. (Within the terms of this report. 'fertility regulation' means contraception, sterilisation and abortion.)

Clinics in Schools

The revised guidance on sex and relationship education, issued in July 2000 by the Department for Education and Employment, was characterised by the same tension found in earlier documents between respect for parental responsibility on the one hand, and treating children as autonomous individuals on the other. The guidance suggests that in any confidential consultation, a health professional will encourage the young person to talk to his or her parents and insists that:

> It is only in the most exceptional case that schools should be in the position of having to handle such information [that a pupil is having, or contemplating having, sexual intercourse] without parental knowledge, and where younger pupils were involved this would be grounds for serious concern.[98]

However, the same document leaves the door wide open to the provision of contraceptive advice and supplies to young people under the age of consent to sexual intercourse by health professionals operating on school premises:

> Health professionals who are involved in delivering programmes are expected to work within the school's sex and relationship education policy and on the instructions of the head teacher. However, when they are in their professional role, such as a school nurse in a consultation with an individual pupil, they should follow their own professional codes of conduct (this is the case irrespective of who is paying them). A school's sex and relationship education policy must make this clear to parents.[99]

> Outside the teaching situation, health professionals such as school nurses can:

> • give one-to-one advice or information to a pupil on a health-related matter including contraception; and

> • exercise their own professional judgment as to whether a young person has the maturity to consent to medical treatment including contraceptive treatment. (The criteria for making such a decision

---

[98] Department for Education and Employment (2000), *Sex and Relationship Education Guidance*, Circular 0116/2000, para 7.10,13.

[99] *Ibid.*, para 6.4.

are based on the 'Fraser guidelines' and can be found in guidance issued jointly by the Health Education Authority, the British Medical Association, Brook Advisory Centres and others. Any competent young person, regardless of age, can independently seek medical advice and give valid consent to treatment).[100]

The provision of contraceptive drugs in schools without parental knowledge or consent is at variance with the government's 'good practice guide' with regard to the supply of medical treatment to pupils. Official guidance states that there should be 'prior written agreement from parents or guardians for any medication, prescribed or non-prescription, to be given to a child' and that:

> School staff should generally not give non-prescribed medication to pupils [e.g. aspirin and paracetamol]. They may not know whether the pupil has taken a previous dose, or whether the medication may react with other medication being taken. **A child under 12 should never be given aspirin, unless prescribed** by a doctor . . .
>
> No pupil under 16 should be given medication without his or her parent's written consent.[101] *(emphasis in original)*

However, school nurses employed by the health authority rather than by the school are not bound by education legislation and guidance, thus providing a mechanism to circumvent the government's 'good practice guide' and permit the contraceptive pill and the morning-after pill to be made available to pupils without the knowledge or consent of their parents. This loophole has been exploited in a number of regions by health authorities which have set up advice clinics in schools. For example, since

---

[100] *Ibid.*, para 7.16.

[101] Department for Education & Employment, Department of Health. *Supporting Pupils with Medical Needs: A good practice guide.* London: HMSO 1996.

1997, nineteen Bodyzone health clinics have been set up in Oxfordshire, serving a population of around 20,000 young people, sixteen clinics being based in schools.[102] The project pack explains that the family planning nurse can '...issue condoms, emergency contraception and repeat supplies of the pill and injectables without a doctor present'.[103]

Young people as young as 11 attending a Bodyzone clinic are issued with a welcome form which assures them that 'this is a completely CONFIDENTIAL service . . . your school/college are not allowed to ask why you are attending Bodyzone'. The first option on the form is for children to ask for 'the sexual health nurse (for contraception, pregnancy tests, supplies and advice)'. Similar schemes have been set up in other parts of the country, some of them based on the Bodyzone model.

Linking Schools and Sexual Health Services

In April 2003, the Sex Education Forum published a booklet designed to encourage secondary schools to forge closer links with agencies providing specialist sexual health advice and support and to give guidance on improving young people's access to sexual health services both within the school and in the wider community.[104] The booklet was commissioned by the Teenage Pregnancy Unit. It notes that:

> improving uptake of sexual health advice, support and services is one of the key aims of the Teenage Pregnancy Strategy . . . The Teenage Pregnancy Strategy stresses the importance of reassuring young people about their entitlement to receive contraceptive advice in confidence within the established legal framework. This is seen as a

---

[102] Government Office for the South East, *Partnership Working Toolkit*, Guildford 2003.

[103] Bodyzone Information Pack 2.

[104] Sarah Thistle, *Secondary schools and sexual health services: Forging the links*, Sex Education Forum, London 2003.

key factor in helping to achieve the strategy's goal of reducing the conception rate in under-18s by 50 per cent by 2010.[105]

The major part of the booklet outlines various practical ways that schools may use to forge links with local sexual health services. The aim is 'to either increase young people's uptake of services in the community or to broaden what is offered on school premises', success being measured in terms of how many young people access the service. There is no suggestion of aiming to influence the behaviour of young people in such a way as to reduce their need for those services in the first place. The goals are both limited and short-sighted, grounded in a fatalistic attitude towards the sexual behaviour of young people.

In an attempt to allay fears about the introduction of sexual health clinics in schools, it is emphasised that they are simply 'extending access rather than providing something new':

> It is useful to remind ourselves that young people, including under-16s, are already legally entitled to free sexual health advice and support, as well as contraceptive services, from: NHS contraceptive / family planning clinics; Brook and other young people's advisory clinics; their own GP...; another GP by asking to register for contraceptive/family planning services only; NHS walk-in centres; young people's information / 'one stop' shops; GUM / STI clinics; some pharmacists providing free emergency contraception under NHS arrangements, using patient group directions...; some community outreach services; some youth centres, foster and learning care projects; Connexions projects and initiatives.[106]

Reference is made to the 'Fraser Guidelines', but at no point is it mentioned that Lord Fraser, one of the Law Lords ruling on Mrs

---

[105] *Ibid.*, p.4

[106] *Ibid.*, p.18

Gillick's case (see p.47), was at pains to stress that the provision of contraception to young people under the age of 16 without parental knowledge and consent should be a 'most unusual' occurrence.[107] Lord Fraser emphasised that his ruling against a total ban on the provision of contraception to a girl under the age of consent:

> ought not to be regarded as a licence for doctors to disregard the wishes of parents on this matter whenever they find it convenient to do so. Any doctor who behaves in such a way would, in my opinion, be failing to discharge his professional responsibilities, and I would expect him to be disciplined by his own professional body accordingly.[108]

Yet, in the space of less than two decades, with the encouragement of the government and spurred on by the health and sex education establishment, the exception has become the norm and parents are increasingly being marginalised. Indeed, a toolkit for general practice, primary care groups and trusts, developed and published by the Royal College of General Practitioners and Brook in 2000 with funding from the Department of Health and the Teenage Pregnancy Unit, expressed concern that young people's fears about confidentiality is a major deterrent to their seeking sexual health advice. Endorsed by the Royal College of General Practitioners, the General Practitioners Committee, the British Medical Association, the Royal College of Nursing and the Medical Defence Union, the resource set out 'to address the needs of all patients by helping general practices reinforce confidentiality as the cornerstone of their services' irrespective of age:

---

[107] Gillick v West Norfolk and Wisbech Area Health Authority and another – [1985] 3 All ER 402.

[108] *Ibid.*

The duty of confidentiality owed to a young person is as great as the duty owed to any other person.[109]

While the 'toolkit' suggests that young people, particularly those under the age of 16, should be encouraged to involve their parents or another appropriate person in decisions about their health and care, it goes on to say that if they refuse to do so, their wishes should be respected, the only exception being if there appears to be grave risk to their welfare.[110] Medical practices are encouraged to develop their own confidentiality policy, clearly stating that the duty of confidentiality is owed to all patients, including those under the age of 16.[111]

It is also recommended that practices draw up a confidentiality statement which is brought to the attention of their patients. A sample statement assures patients:

> You can be sure that anything you discuss with any member of this practice – family doctor, nurse or receptionist – will stay confidential. Even if you are under 16, nothing will be said to anyone – including parents, other family members, care workers or tutors – without your permission.[112]

The 'toolkit' commends the example of practices which have gone out of their way to invite teenagers as young as 13 or 14 to a confidential consultation without their parents present:

> Some practices have successfully taken a proactive approach – sending a leaflet or birthday card to teenage patients on their thirteenth or fourteenth birthday and inviting them to the surgery for a confidential consultation on any aspect of their health. These

---

[109] Royal College of General Practitioners and Brook, *Confidentiality and young people: Improving teenagers' uptake of sexual and other health advice*, 2000

[110] *Ibid.*, p.18

[111] *Ibid.*, p.15, 17

[112] *Ibid.*, p.22

initiatives have been welcomed by both young people and their parents…

For young people under 16 the consultation is an opportunity to inform and reassure them about practice confidentiality as well as to offer them the option of being seen on their own without a parent or carer.[113]

Confidential consultations are now being encouraged by health professionals to the extent that the president of the Royal College of Paediatrics and Child Health could state on public record that it would be perfectly reasonable for a GP to provide contraceptive advice and treatment in confidence to a 12-year-old girl who was involved in a sexual relationship with a 22-year-old man. Notwithstanding the fact that the law regards such a relationship as statutory rape with a maximum sentence of life imprisonment, Professor David Hall told the Joint Committee on Human Rights that, provided the GP judged that the girl was making a mature and considered opinion in seeking professional advice, he or she 'would probably give her the advice that she was requesting because' she would be considered 'very competent by the very act of having come to seek advice on contraception'.[114]

The zeal for preserving confidentiality at virtually all costs has led to a situation where parents are being excluded from decisions that vitally affect their children's lives. The provision of contraceptive advice and supplies to young people under the age of consent serves to break down relationships of trust within the family and establish in their place bonds with service providers whose interest is professional rather than personal. The pursuit of 'the sexual rights' of children and young people has deprived them of the protective instincts and influence of

---

[113] *Ibid.*, p.22

[114] Joint Committee on Human Rights, *The Case for a Human Rights Commission: Interim Report*, Twenty-second Report of Session 2001-02, HL Paper 160, HC 1142, Ev60, para 284.

their parents and exposed them to the risk of sexual exploitation, emotional trauma and physical disease with, in some cases, lifelong consequences.

Chapter 8

What of the future?

The British public is repeatedly told that nationwide sex education and the provision of contraceptives to teenagers are justified by the need to bring down the number of unwanted pregnancies. The whole exercise has been a colossal failure. Under-16 conception and abortion rates have witnessed only very minor annual fluctuations during the past decade with little change overall. Britain still has the highest teenage pregnancy rate in Western Europe. Official government advisors are now openly acknowledging that rising rates of STIs have reached crisis proportions and the problem is rapidly going down the age range, with massive increases in the incidence of gonorrhoea and chlamydia among teenage women due to early and promiscuous sexual activity. Yet the same policies are pursued relentlessly: more sex education, more explicit, and at younger ages; more contraceptives supplied at more sex clinics, to be followed by more abortions.

Dr Malcolm Potts, who has acted as a consultant to many organisations involved with contraception and family health and served as the first medical director of the IPPF, admitted years ago that this would be the case: 'As people turn to contraception, there will be a rise, not a fall, in the abortion rate'.[115] And again, 'No society has controlled its fertility . . . without recourse to a significant number of abortions. In fact abortion is often the starting place in the control of fertility'.[116]

The reason has become obvious over the years: contraception and abortion are inextricably bound together. One

---

[115] Report, *Cambridge Evening News*, 7 February 1973.

[116] Malcolm Potts, 'Fertility Rights', *The Guardian*, 25 April 1979.

70

physician and researcher for the Brook Advisory Centres has confirmed this:

> Twenty years ago women were more resigned to unwanted pregnancy, but as they have become more conscious of preventing conception, so they have come to request terminations when contraception fails. There is overwhelming evidence that, contrary to what you might expect, *the availability of contraception leads to an increase in the abortion rate.*[117] (*emphasis added*)

In a similar vein, a working party of the Royal College of Obstetricians on unplanned pregnancy observed that: 'the increased efficiency and availability of contraception may lower people's tolerance for unplanned pregnancy.'[118]

The reason why youngsters and the public at large are not told the truth is clear. Even though research (carried out by people sympathetic to the birth control lobby) has found that sexual experience in young people lessens the importance of parental influence,[119] the same policies are pursued because nothing must thwart the ideology of liberating children from their families. The end justifies the means.

In this book I have sought to expose some of the hidden connivances, implications, and activities of an interlocking power structure of which sex education is one – but by no means the only – concern. It is a lobby which has been described as 'one of the most savagely damaging lobbies a society has ever had to confront'.[120] It is damaging because the sex education it seeks to promote (under whatever guise it may appear) is a vehicle to spread an amoralism that is destructive of the family and of society.

---

[117] Judith Bury, 'Sex Education for Bureaucrats', *The Scotsman*, 29 June 1981.

[118] Report of the RCOG Working Party on Unplanned Pregnancy. Royal College of Obstetricians and Gynaecologists. London, 1991, p.10.

[119] Christine Farrell, *My Mother Said,* Routledge and Kegan Paul, 1978

[120] Patrick Cosgrave, 'The Politics of Sex Education', *The Spectator*, 31 August 1974.

When a nation is threatened with enemies from outside or confronted with economic policies which may damage future national stability, there is public controversy, advocacy of solutions and the emergence of alternative strategies and policies which are adopted or rejected on the basis of their demonstrable effectiveness. Where matters of family policy and social mores are concerned, however, political and public debate seems to become stricken with paralysis, closed to scrutiny, and fearful of the word 'morality'. Yet the issue at stake concerns the fabric of society and the very future of the human race. The threat posed should command an immediate response, energetic debate and the formation of counter-policies.

It is imperative that people of good will investigate and unravel the strands which have been cleverly woven round the policies, laws and institutions in their own countries. The instigators need to be identified and exposed, because they function with impunity, in secrecy or behind a screen of pseudo-respectability afforded by government funding for their activities and policies.

It is an awesome situation to contemplate and act upon. It is one which requires coordinated effort by those who believe in and support the family and the sanctity of human life. It is a battle to be fought now by those who cherish the true meaning of freedom.

Glossary of Acronyms

CMO	Chief Medical Officer
CRDU	Children's Rights Development Unit
DfEE	Department for Education and Employment
FPA	Family Planning Association
IAG	Independent Advisory Group on Teenage Pregnancy
IPPF	International Planned Parenthood Federation
NCB	National Children's Bureau
PSHE	Personal Social and Health Education
SEF	Sex Education Forum
SEU	Social Exclusion Unit
SIECUS	Sex Information and Education Council of the United States
SRE	Sex and Relationships Education
STI	Sexually Transmitted Infection
TPU	Teenage Pregnancy Unit

Index